AF226128

For Alana,
continue having
great adventures!

"Mommy, I think I want to be a firefighter when I grow up." Alana said one morning while eating her toast.

"A firefighter?" laughed her older brother Alex. "Only boys do that job."

"Now Alex," said their father. "That's not true. Girls all over the world are firefighters."

"Yeah, right." said Alex, rolling his eyes.

Alana's mother pointed to the big round clock on the wall. 8 o'clock. "Time for school. Grab your backpacks and don't forget your lunch." She smiled and handed them their lunch boxes.

"Bye Dad." Alana waved to her father. "Bye Simba" She waved to her dog.

The dress-up chest in Alana's room gave her mother a super idea.

She climbed up the narrow stairs to the attic and found what she was looking for...
the Halloween costume box. She was thrilled to find a red firefighter hat,
a shiny yellow rain coat, plastic goggles and a small black rubber hose.

She gathered them in her arms and placed the items inside the chest at the foot of
Alana's bed.

Later on, in the middle of the night, an owl hooting in a tree outside woke Alana up. She saw that her dress-up chest was open.

She pulled back the blankets, crawled out of bed and looked inside. **There was a red firefighter hat on top!**

CALIFORNIA REPUBLIC

"What's this?" Alana wondered as she put on the hat and the yellow jacket. Alana grabbed the hose in both hands and suddenly she was stepping out of a huge red fire truck with bright flashing lights and loud sirens blasting.

There was a very tall building nearby burning brightly with flames roaring out the windows.

"Turn on the water!" Alana yelled as she aimed the hose up high. Water sprayed in all directions and she began to sweat with the fiery heat.

Alana lifted her arms to shield her face when thick black clouds of smoke blew at her. She coughed and tried not to breathe the dark and choking air.

One of the firefighters screamed from the fire truck. "Go for it!"

She grabbed her mask and pointed the hose at the fire. The flames soon died down. The building was black, crisp and filled with blinding smoke, but the fire was finally out.

"Well done Alana! You were fantastic." Everyone around her patted her on the back.

Exhausted from her work as a firefighter, Alana climbed into her bed and went back to sleep.

The next morning Alana looked around her room and the chest was closed.
There was no firefighter outfit anywhere. She didn't know what to think.

"Mommy! Daddy!" Alana said. "Last night I dreamed I was a
firefighter and put out a raging fire in a humongous
big building. Everyone said I did great."

"Ha! Did you get burned?" Her brother Alex snarled.
"No." Alana said shaking her head.
"But it was boiling hot and soooo smoky.
It was cool to put out such a big fire and
help save lives but... maybe I could be
something else.

Alana thought for a moment. "How about a builder? I could make beautiful houses and gorgeous buildings and big towers just like the Eiffel Tower in Paris. And even make houses for people that have no homes."

"No way!" said her brother Alex. "Only boys do that kind of job. I've never seen a girl driving huge cranes or big diggers. Have you Mom?" Alex asked.

"Well, just yesterday I saw a few women wearing hard hats working beside men on a building site in the city. Girls can be architects who design the building or engineers who make sure the building is safe or even project managers who are in charge of all the workers on the job."

"I bet I could do that." Alana smiled.

In the middle of the night, Alana woke up and saw that her chest was open again with a bright yellow hard hat on top.

She crawled out of bed and placed it on her head and tucked her hair up inside it. Alana looked down and saw a large notepad with a pencil hanging from it and a thick brown belt with pockets filled with tools.

There was a hammer, some screwdrivers, a flashlight and a measuring tape. Alana placed the belt around her waist, fastened it and looked in the mirror.

"Wow!" She said out loud and closed her eyes. **Suddenly she was standing on a narrow beam in a tall building high above the ground.** There were workers everywhere; hammering, sawing, drilling and shouting to one another. All the noise hurt her ears.

"Alana!" A man called and pointed to a glass window being lifted in place. "What do you think?"

Another tapped her on the shoulder and asked her to look at some drawings and handed her the phone. "Here, it's the architect. She needs to talk to you. Now!"

Alana didn't now what to do first. Then she looked down and started to wobble.

"Yikes!" She yelled and grabbed onto the pole next to her. It was such a long drop down to the pavement.

"What am I doing here?" She wondered. "Only birds and airplanes should be this high up in the sky. This is NOT for me."

She opened her eyes and was happy to see she was back in her bedroom. She took off the hat and removed the belt full of tools and climbed back into her bed and fell asleep.

When the sun poked its warm light through her window, Alana rubbed her eyes and walked downstairs to the kitchen and turned to her mommy and daddy.

"Last night I had a dream that I was a builder and I was standing very high up in a very tall building. It was so tall it almost touched the sky. It was sooooooo noisy up there and everyone kept shouting things at me. I got really scared when I looked down all the way to the ground. It would be fun to design and build houses or offices that people would love but I think I might like to do something else.

Uh, maybe a fighter pilot? I could land planes on top of those giant Navy ships."

"Oh please." said her brother. "There's no way girls can do that job. And they're called aircraft carriers, silly, not ships."

"I'm not silly." She pouted.

Her father smiled at her. "Well honey, girls like you should always try to do something if that's what they really want, even if it seems a bit scary at first. You must be brave and stick with it. And Alex, you need to stop being so closed-minded.

When Alana and Alex were at school, their mother drove to the Salvation Army shop and looked through the racks of clothes for some ideas. **She was in luck! There was a navy blue jumpsuit.**

She brought it home and worked on it all morning; measuring, cutting and sewing it to make it fit Alana's little body. When she finally finished, she held up a perfect fighter pilot uniform for Alana. But something was missing. Of course, the sunglasses! She grabbed a pair of old sunglasses with a gold rim and placed the outfit inside Alana's chest.

That night, once again, Alana woke up and her chest was open. She saw a navy blue jumpsuit and pulled it on over her pajamas, zipped up the front and reached down for the sunglasses and slipped them on.

Alana climbed into the jet and fastened the harness. She stared down at all the buttons and switches on the control panel in the jet. She looked out the window, gave a big thumbs-up and pressed the button to start the engine.

She placed her foot firmly on the pedal and tore down the runway on the ship into the clear blue sky. When she looked out the window, the ship looked like a huge floating monster sitting on the ocean and her heart began to beat faster.

"You can do this." She whispered to herself.

"Okay. Ready for approach." The radio called to her. "Just take it nice and slow now."

Alana flew over the ship and made a big sweeping circle in the sky keeping her eyes on the runway below her. She lowered the nose of the jet and slowed it down.

"Oh no!" She screamed. "I'm far too high. I'm not going to make it." She asked permission to circle one more time.

This time she landed perfectly and everyone cheered.

She took off her helmet and felt her heart pounding hard and she was covered in sweat.

"Wow! Alana said the
next morning. "Last
night I dreamed I
was a fighter pilot
and landed my jet
perfectly onto a big
ship floating in the
ocean. It was very
exciting but I like to
be around people and
not up in the sky all
by myself."

She looked over at her
little dog, Simba.
Maybe I can be an
animal doctor and
take care of sick
pets, right Dad?"

"Indeed."
Her father smiled.

"Alana," Her mother said. "You can do many jobs in your life. And even be your own boss, if you'd like. **You can always change what you do, but not what you love.**" Alana thought about this a minute.

"I want to do so many things. I just don't know."
"Well, why don't you just be yourself for now?" Her daddy hugged her.
"And right now, it's time for school. Off you go and brush your teeth." Her mommy said.

That night Alana did not wake up. The first thing she saw in the morning was a pink ballet costume and soft pink slippers with white ribbons sitting on top of her dress-up chest.

"Yes! Today I start my dance classes. It's going to be so much fun."

She tried on the ballet outfit and looked in the mirror. It fit perfectly.

Then she put her feet into the soft pink slippers and held her arms high above her head until both hands touched and **twirled around and around in circles until she felt dizzy and hungry.**

Alana went to the kitchen for breakfast. "Thank you so much for my dance classes and beautiful slippers, Mommy. I love them. You're the best mommy." She gave her mother a big hug and looked up at her.

"I think I know what I want to be when I grow up." Alana said.

"Oh? Do tell." Her father smiled.

"It's something only girls can be." Alana said.

"Oh yeah? What's that?" Her brother Alex asked.

"A mommy." Alana smiled.

"A mommy?" Her mother looked over her. "Yes. A mommy. I want to have babies and take care of them. I can get one of those robot machines to do the vacuuming like we have, right Mom? And maybe there will be other robots that can do all the cleaning."

"Wouldn't that be wonderful! Well, being a mommy is certainly one of the most rewarding jobs, Alana. But you can be a mommy and do something else you love as well." Her mother promised.

"Maybe a famous ballerina?
And a pet doctor too?" Alana wondered.

Her mother and father smiled.

"I'm going to wear my new pink slippers and practice all day."
Alana promised and stood on her tippy toes and danced out
of the room.

Proceeds from book sales will be donated
to an Armenian relief fund and orphanage.

For other books
by Susan C Sahakian,
please visit the author's website
susanctunney.com

ISBN 978-0-473-54977-0 (softcover)
ISBN 978-0-473-54978-7 (hardcover)